Animal Top Tens

North America's Most Amazing Animals

Anita Ganeri

Chicago, Illinois

Photo Research: Mica Brancic
Editorial: Nancy Dickmann and Catherine Veitch
Design: Victoria Bevan and Geoff Ward
Illustrations: Geoff Ward
Production: Victoria Fitzgerald

Originated by Modern Age
Printed and bound by CTPS (China Translation
& Printing Services Ltd)

12 11 10 09 08
10 9 8 7 6 5 4 3 2 1

Library of Congress Cataloging-in-Publication Data
Ganeri, Anita, 1961-
   North America's most amazing animals / Anita Ganeri.
      p. cm. -- (Animal top tens)
   Includes bibliographical references and index.
   ISBN 978-1-4109-3087-3 (hc) -- ISBN 978-1-4109-3096-5 (pb) I. Animals--North America--Juvenile literature. I. Title.
   QL151.G36 2008
   591.97--dc22
                                    2007047553

Acknowledgments
The author and publisher are grateful to the following for permission to reproduce copyright material: ©Ardea pp. **4, 9, 13, 22, 24** (Tom & Pat Leeson), **19, 27** (John Cancalosi); ©Corbis p. **11** (Ralph A. Clevenger); ©FLPA p. **21** (David Hosking); ©FLPA/Minden Pictures pp. **7** (Michael Quinton), **20** (Jim Brandenburg), **23** (Sumio Harada); ©FLPA/Minden Pictures/ZSSD pp. **14, 17**; ©NHPA p. **10** (John Shaw); ©OSF pp. **15** (Patricio Robles Gil), **16** (Michael Fogden), **25** (Densey Clyne); ©OSF/Alaska Stock Images p. **8** (Bruce J. Lichtenberger); ©OSF/Earth Scenes/Animals Animals p. **18** (David M. Dennis); ©OSF/Ifa-Bilderteam Gmbh p. **6**; ©OSF/Index Stock Imagery p. **12** (Mark Drewelow); ©OSF/Pacific Stock p. **26** (Perrine Doug).

Cover photograph of a bull moose, reproduced with permission of PhotoLibrary/Brunner Eberhard.

The publisher would like to thank Michael Bright for his assistance in the preparation of this book.

Every effort has been made to contact copyright holders of any material reproduced in this book. Any omissions will be rectified in subsequent printings if notice is given to the publishers.

Disclaimer
All the internet addresses (URLs) given in this book were valid at time of going to press. However, due to the dynamic nature of the Internet, some addresses may have changed, or sites may have changed or ceased to exist since publication. While the author and publishers regret any inconvenience this may cause readers, no responsibility for any such changes can be accepted by either the author or the publishers. It is recommended that adults supervise children on the Internet.

Contents

Some words are printed in bold, **like this**. You can find out what they mean in the Glossary.

North America

North America is the world's third largest **continent**. It covers just over 9 million square miles (24 million square kilometers). North America stretches from Canada in the north to Mexico in the south, and from the Pacific Ocean in the west to the Atlantic Ocean in the east. A large number of islands lie off the coast.

North America has many different types of landscapes. The Rocky Mountains run from Alaska in the north to New Mexico in the south. The Great Lakes, on the border between the United States and Canada, include the largest **freshwater** lake in the world. There are also enormous rivers, such as the Mississippi and Missouri, and vast deserts and forests.

The Rocky Mountains stretch for 3,000 miles (4,800 kilometers).

This map shows some of the main landscapes of North America.

Key
- conifer forest
- desert
- mountains

N
W—E
S

0 | 1000 miles
0 | 1000 kilometers

Alaska

CANADA

Pacific Ocean

Rocky Mountains

Missouri River

Great Lakes

UNITED STATES

Appalachian Mountains

Mississippi River

Atlantic Ocean

Sonoran Desert

The Everglades

Mexico

North America

An amazing range of animals has **adapted** to live in the **habitats** of North America. Grizzly bears and mountain lions live among the mountains. The dry deserts are home to snakes, tortoises, and lizards. Thick **coniferous** forests shelter moose, beavers, and eagles. These animals have special features that help them survive in their particular homes.

Bald Eagle

The bald eagle is a large **bird of prey**. It has brown feathers and a white head and tail. Its beak, feet, and eyes are bright yellow.

BALD EAGLE

BODY LENGTH:
OVER 31 IN. (80 CM)

WINGSPAN:
OVER 6.5 FT. (2 M)

WEIGHT:
7–14 LBS
(3.1–6.2 KG)

LIFESPAN:
20–30 YEARS

HABITAT:
NEAR COASTS, LAKE SHORES, AND RIVERBANKS

THAT'S AMAZING!:
BALD EAGLES ARE NOT ACTUALLY BALD. BALD IS AN OLD WORD MEANING "WHITE."

North America

Pacific Ocean

Atlantic Ocean

□ where bald eagles live

Eagle comeback

About 50 years ago, bald eagles were in danger of dying out. A chemical that farmers sprayed on their crops kept the eagles from **mating** properly and laying healthy eggs. Since then, people have worked hard to save the eagles, with great success. Recently, the bald eagle was officially removed from the list of animals in danger of becoming **extinct**.

Bald eagles are excellent at catching fish.

Bald eagles build huge nests in trees near water.

Habitat and hunting

Bald eagles live in forests near water. Here there are plenty of fish to eat and tall trees to roost and nest in. They swoop low over the water and grab fish using their sharp **talons**.

Sea Otter

Sea otters live in the Pacific Ocean off the west coast of North America. They spend most of their time in the water, and have **streamlined** bodies and webbed back feet to help them swim. An otter spends up to three hours each day grooming its thick fur coat. This helps trap a layer of air among the long hairs. The air keeps the otter warm in the icy-cold water.

Sea otters live among beds of giant kelp seaweed.

SEA OTTER

BODY LENGTH:
4–5 FT. (1.2–1.5 M)

WEIGHT:
50–100 LBS (22–45 KG)

LIFESPAN:
AVERAGE 10–11 YEARS

HABITAT:
ROCKY COASTS

THAT'S AMAZING!:
AT NIGHT, A SEA OTTER WRAPS
A LONG PIECE OF SEAWEED
AROUND ITS BODY TO KEEP IT
FROM BEING WASHED AWAY.

North
America

Pacific
Ocean

Atlantic
Ocean

where sea otters live

Sea otters feed, float, swim, and sleep on their backs.

Using tools

A sea otter feeds on sea urchins and clams. It dives down
to the sea floor to catch them and brings them back to the
surface. Then it lies on its back and balances a flat stone on
its chest. It smashes a shellfish against the stone to open
it up to eat. An otter keeps a favorite stone in a fold of
skin under its armpit.

Grizzly Bear

The massive grizzly bear lives in mountains and **coniferous** forests. It gets its name from the white-tipped hairs on its shoulders and neck. These hairs give its brown fur a grizzled appearance.

GRIZZLY BEAR

BODY LENGTH:
6–9 FT. (1.8–2.8 M)

WEIGHT:
UP TO 900 LBS (400 KG)

LIFESPAN:
20–30 YEARS

HABITAT:
MOUNTAINS, CONIFEROUS FORESTS

THAT'S AMAZING!:
GRIZZLY BEAR CUBS ARE BORN IN THEIR MOTHER'S DEN IN THE MIDDLE OF WINTER.

North America

Pacific Ocean

Atlantic Ocean

where grizzly bears live

Grizzly bears use their huge paws to fish for salmon.

Seasonal food

Grizzly bears eat a wide range of food, depending on the time of year. In fall, for example, they mostly eat berries, fruit, nuts, roots, and bulbs. They also hunt animals, such as moose, bison, sheep, and fish. Although the bears are big, they can run fast after **prey** and kill it with a swipe from their paws. A muscle in their shoulders gives extra strength to their huge arms.

Winter sleep

Grizzly bears sleep through the winter when food is scarce. Their breathing and heart rate slows down and their body temperature drops. They live off fat stored in their bodies. This is called **hibernating**.

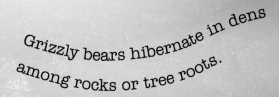

Grizzly bears hibernate in dens among rocks or tree roots.

Rocky Mountain Goat

Rocky Mountain goats live high in the Rocky and Cascade Mountains of North America, at heights of more than 10,000 feet (3,000 meters). Mountain goats are perfectly **adapted** to their mountain life. Thick, wool coats protect them from the cold and wind. Their coats get thicker in winter when temperatures can fall as low as -50 °F (-46 °C). In summer, mountain goats shed their coats by rubbing themselves against the rocks.

Rocky Mountain goats have long horns and beards.

ROCKY MOUNTAIN GOAT

HEIGHT AT SHOULDER:
UP TO 3.3 FT. (1 M)

WEIGHT:
ON AVERAGE 200 LBS
(90 KG)

LIFESPAN:
12–15 YEARS

HABITAT:
MOUNTAINS

THAT'S AMAZING!:
BABY MOUNTAIN GOATS CAN
STAND UP MINUTES AFTER THEY
ARE BORN AND CLIMB STEEP
SLOPES A FEW DAYS LATER.

North America

Pacific Ocean

Atlantic Ocean

where Rocky Mountain goats live

The mountain goat's white coat helps it hide in the winter snow.

High climbers

The mountain goats' feet are well suited for climbing the
mountain slopes. Their hooves have a hard outer edge for digging
into cracks in the rock, and rubber-like pads for a better grip.
This helps the mountain goats cross rocky ground. It also helps
them cling to steep ledges and cliffs where they are safe from
predators, such as wolves and bears.

Sidewinder

The sidewinder is a rattlesnake that lives in the **deserts** of the southwestern United States. It has several special features to help it live in its harsh **habitat**. Its skin is tan with brown and yellow blotches. This coloring **camouflages** the sidewinder as it lies half-buried in the sand. It waits for its **prey** of **rodents** and lizards to pass by. Then it strikes with a poisonous bite.

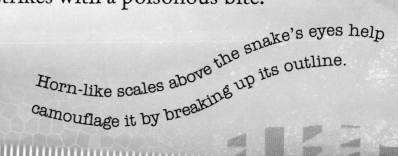

Horn-like scales above the snake's eyes help camouflage it by breaking up its outline.

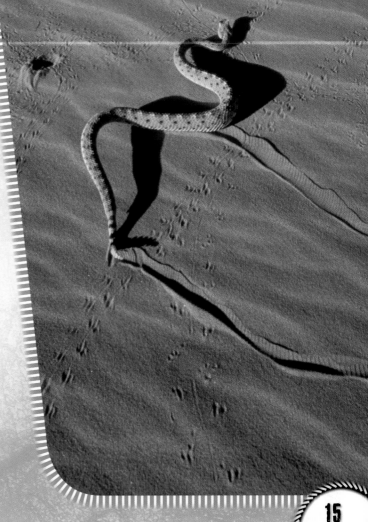

SIDEWINDER

BODY LENGTH:
23–28 IN. (53–71 CM)

WEIGHT:
4–10 LBS (1.8–4.5 KG)

LIFESPAN:
20–30 YEARS
(IN **CAPTIVITY**)

HABITAT:
DESERTS

THAT'S AMAZING!:
RATTLESNAKES ARE FAMOUS FOR THE RATTLES AT THE TIPS OF THEIR TAILS. THEY SHAKE THESE TO WARN OFF **PREDATORS**. THE RATTLE IS ACTUALLY A CHAIN OF SCALES.

North America

Pacific Ocean

Atlantic Ocean

where sidewinders live

The sidewinder gets its name from the way it moves over the sand.

Slithering over sand

The sidewinder has an unusual way of moving. It throws its body sideways in a series of loops. This allows the snake to grip the loose, slippery sand so that it can pull itself along. It means that the snake's body hardly touches the hot sand and does not get burned.

15

Gila Monster

The gila monster is a large lizard with a large head and short tail. It lives in the **deserts** of the southwestern United States. Its skin feels bumpy because it is covered in small, bony scales. Its black and pink colors help **camouflage** it among the rocks and sand. They also warn its **predators** that it is poisonous.

GILA MONSTER

BODY LENGTH:
UP TO 23 IN. (58 CM)

WEIGHT:
4 LBS (1.8 KG)

LIFESPAN:
UP TO 20 YEARS
(IN **CAPTIVITY**)

HABITAT:
DESERTS

THAT'S AMAZING!:
GILA MONSTERS
SOMETIMES DIG
THEIR OWN **BURROWS**.
SOMETIMES THEY STEAL
OTHER ANIMALS' BURROWS.

North America

Pacific Ocean

Atlantic Ocean

where gila monsters live

The gila monster hunts for food at dusk, when it is cooler.

Catching food

Food is hard to find in the desert. Because of this, gila monsters eat a large amount at one time and only need three to four meals a year. They store fat in their tails to use when there is no food. They feed on small **rodents**, young birds, and birds' eggs. When a gila monster bites its **prey**, poison flows along grooves in its lower teeth.

A gila monster's claws are great for digging burrows, and for digging up other animals' eggs.

American Alligator

The American alligator is one of the world's largest **reptiles**. It is **adapted** for life in the water. Its olive-green coloring makes good **camouflage** and it uses its long, muscular tail for swimming.

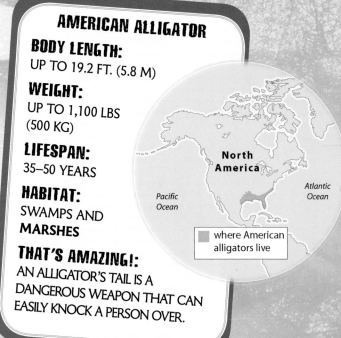

AMERICAN ALLIGATOR

BODY LENGTH:
UP TO 19.2 FT. (5.8 M)

WEIGHT:
UP TO 1,100 LBS (500 KG)

LIFESPAN:
35–50 YEARS

HABITAT:
SWAMPS AND **MARSHES**

THAT'S AMAZING!:
AN ALLIGATOR'S TAIL IS A DANGEROUS WEAPON THAT CAN EASILY KNOCK A PERSON OVER.

North America

Pacific Ocean

Atlantic Ocean

where American alligators live

Alligators often lie or bask in the sun in warm weather. If the day gets too hot they move to a shady spot.

Water holes

During the dry season, the swamps dry up. An alligator digs a large hole in the floor of the **swamp**. This fills up with water in the wet season and stays full when the rains stop. It also fills up with turtles, fish, and snakes that give the alligator its food.

The Everglades

The Everglades is an enormous swamp in southern Florida. Most of the swamp is covered in a plant called sawgrass, with a few trees. Deep channels of water run through it. The Everglades is a rich **mating** and feeding ground for many fish, insects, reptiles, and birds.

The American alligator lives in swamps in the southeastern United States.

Beaver

Beavers are large **rodents** that live in streams and lakes near forests. They are very well **adapted** to their life in and around the water. Their back feet are webbed for swimming and they use their paddle-like tails to steer. Their coats are sleek and waterproof, and they can hold their breath for up to 15 minutes when they dive.

It takes a beaver just a few minutes to bite through a thick branch.

Master builders

Beavers are clever builders. They use their strong jaws and large front teeth to gnaw through tree trunks and cut them into logs. Then they use the logs and mud to build a **dam** across a stream to form a pond. In the pond, they build a wooden lodge to live in. They reach the lodge through underwater tunnels. The tunnels help keep out **predators,** such as bears or wolves.

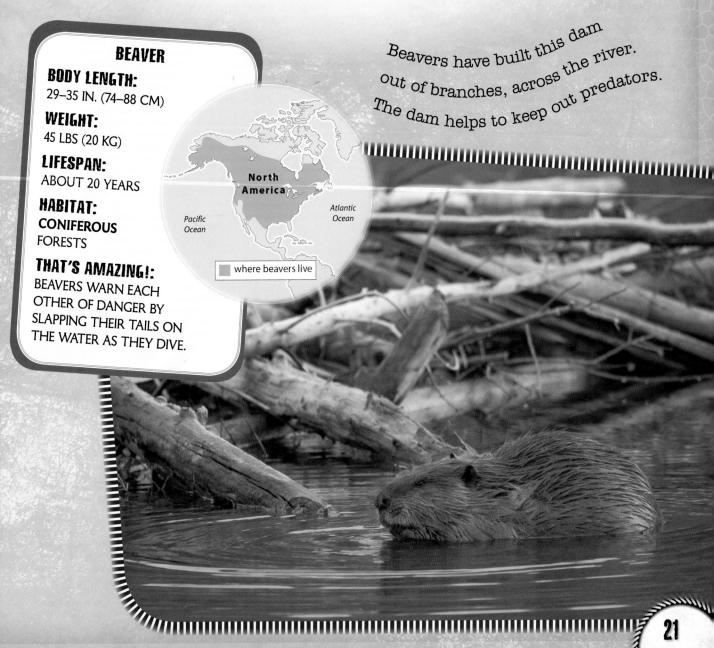

BEAVER

BODY LENGTH:
29–35 IN. (74–88 CM)

WEIGHT:
45 LBS (20 KG)

LIFESPAN:
ABOUT 20 YEARS

HABITAT:
CONIFEROUS FORESTS

THAT'S AMAZING!:
BEAVERS WARN EACH OTHER OF DANGER BY SLAPPING THEIR TAILS ON THE WATER AS THEY DIVE.

North America

Pacific Ocean

Atlantic Ocean

☐ where beavers live

Beavers have built this dam out of branches, across the river. The dam helps to keep out predators.

Moose

Moose live in the **coniferous** forests of Alaska, Canada, and the northeastern United States. They are the largest living deer, with large bodies, huge heads, and long noses. The moose's diet changes with the seasons. In summer they eat water plants and in winter they eat the conifer branches of trees such as pine, spruce, and fir. They have special features that make forest life easier.

In winter, their long legs allow them to move through deep snow and their thick coats keep them warm. They are also strong swimmers and sometimes dive into the water to pull up plants from the bottom.

Moose live around **swamps** and lakes in the forest.

MOOSE

HEIGHT AT SHOULDER:
5.5–7.5 FT. (1.7–2.3 M)

WEIGHT:
900–1,600 LBS
(400–725 KG)

LIFESPAN:
UP TO 27 YEARS

HABITAT:
CONIFEROUS FORESTS

THAT'S AMAZING!:
MALE MOOSE HAVE LARGE
FLAPS OF SKIN HANGING UNDER
THEIR THROATS. THESE FLAPS
MAY BE USED IN COURTSHIP.

North
America

Pacific
Ocean

Atlantic
Ocean

where moose live

Antlers

Male moose have huge, crown-shaped antlers that can
measure almost 6.5 feet (2 meters) across. The moose use
their antlers to fight off rival males and attract females for
mating. The moose grow their antlers in the summer, then
shed them in the winter. The antlers take about three to
five months to grow.

Monarch Butterfly

The monarch butterfly is a small butterfly with striking black and orange wings. These bright colors warn **predators** that the butterfly is poisonous to eat. It gets its poison from the milkweed plants it feeds on when it is a caterpillar.

MONARCH BUTTERFLY

BODY LENGTH:
1.3 IN. (3.5 CM)

WEIGHT:
0.02 OZ (0.6 G)

LIFESPAN:
UP TO 8–9 MONTHS

HABITAT:
CONIFEROUS FORESTS (DURING WINTER)

THAT'S AMAZING!:
GENERATION AFTER GENERATION OF MONARCH BUTTERFLIES SPEND THE WINTER IN THE SAME TREES.

where monarch butterflies live

North America

Pacific Ocean

Atlantic Ocean

Some butterflies fly to California. Others fly to Mexico.

Long journey

Some monarch butterflies live in southern Canada and the northern United States. In the fall, millions of these butterflies make an extraordinary journey. They **migrate** more than 2,000 miles (3,200 kilometers) to spend the winter in the south where it is warmer. Otherwise, they would die in the cold. The journey takes them two to three months. In spring, they leave the trees to feed and warm themselves up in the sun. Then they start the long journey north again to **mate**.

The butterflies gather on the branches and trunks of pine and fir trees.

Animals in Danger

Many animals in North America are in danger of dying out. When an animal dies out, it is said to be **extinct**. Many animals are dying out because people are destroying their **habitats**, capturing them for pets, or killing them for their skins, meat, and body parts.

Florida manatees are large sea **mammals** that live off the coast of Florida. They have tough, gray-brown skin and broad, whiskery mouths. Today, the Florida manatee is in danger of dying out. Its habitat is being destroyed by **pollution**. Many manatees also die in accidents with speed boats.

Manatees use their flipper-like arms for swimming and digging up water plants.

California condors live in the mountains of California. Here, they soar above the slopes, looking for dead animals to eat. The California condor is the world's rarest **bird of prey** and there may only be roughly 200 left in the wild. People have put these condors in danger by shooting them and destroying their habitats for new buildings.

Today, **conservation** groups are working hard to save these amazing animals.

California condors are the largest flying birds in North America.

Animal Facts and Figures

There are millions of different types of animals living all over the world. The place where an animal lives is called its **habitat**. Animals have special features, such as wings, claws, and fins. These features allow animals to survive in their habitats. Which animal do you think is the most amazing?

BALD EAGLE

BODY LENGTH:
OVER 31 IN. (80 CM)

WINGSPAN:
OVER 6.5 FT. (2 M)

WEIGHT:
7–14 LBS (3.1–6.2 KG)

LIFESPAN:
20–30 YEARS

HABITAT:
NEAR COASTS, LAKE SHORES, AND RIVERBANKS

THAT'S AMAZING!:
BALD EAGLES ARE NOT ACTUALLY BALD. BALD IS AN OLD WORD MEANING "WHITE."

SEA OTTER

BODY LENGTH:
4–5 FT. (1.2–1.5 M)

WEIGHT:
50–100 LBS (22–45 KG)

LIFESPAN:
AVERAGE 10–11 YEARS

HABITAT:
ROCKY COASTS

THAT'S AMAZING!:
AT NIGHT, A SEA OTTER WRAPS A LONG PIECE OF SEAWEED AROUND ITS BODY TO KEEP IT FROM BEING WASHED AWAY.

GRIZZLY BEAR

BODY LENGTH:
6–9 FT. (1.8–2.8 M)

WEIGHT:
UP TO 900 LBS (400 KG)

LIFESPAN:
20–30 YEARS

HABITAT:
MOUNTAINS, CONIFEROUS FORESTS

THAT'S AMAZING!:
GRIZZLY BEAR CUBS ARE BORN IN THEIR MOTHER'S DEN IN THE MIDDLE OF WINTER.

ROCKY MOUNTAIN GOAT

HEIGHT AT SHOULDER:
UP TO 3.3 FT. (1 M)

WEIGHT:
ON AVERAGE 200 LBS (90 KG)

LIFESPAN:
12–15 YEARS

HABITAT:
MOUNTAINS

THAT'S AMAZING!:
BABY MOUNTAIN GOATS CAN STAND UP MINUTES AFTER THEY ARE BORN AND CLIMB STEEP SLOPES A FEW DAYS LATER.

SIDEWINDER

BODY LENGTH:
23–28 IN. (53–71 CM)

WEIGHT:
4–10 LBS (1.8–4.5 KG)

LIFESPAN:
20–30 YEARS
(IN **CAPTIVITY**)

HABITAT:
DESERTS

THAT'S AMAZING!:
RATTLESNAKES ARE
FAMOUS FOR THE RATTLES
AT THE TIPS OF THEIR TAILS.
THEY SHAKE THESE TO
WARN OFF **PREDATORS**.
THE RATTLE IS ACTUALLY
A CHAIN OF SCALES.

GILA MONSTER

BODY LENGTH:
UP TO 23 IN. (58 CM)

WEIGHT:
4 LBS (1.8 KG)

LIFESPAN:
UP TO 20 YEARS
(IN **CAPTIVITY**)

HABITAT:
DESERTS

THAT'S AMAZING!:
GILA MONSTERS SOMETIMES
DIG THEIR OWN **BURROWS**.
SOMETIMES THEY STEAL
OTHER ANIMALS' BURROWS.

AMERICAN ALLIGATOR

BODY LENGTH:
UP TO 19.2 FT. (5.8 M)

WEIGHT:
UP TO 1,100 LBS (500 KG)

LIFESPAN:
35–50 YEARS

HABITAT:
SWAMPS AND **MARSHES**

THAT'S AMAZING!:
AN ALLIGATOR'S TAIL IS
A DANGEROUS WEAPON
THAT CAN EASILY KNOCK
A PERSON OVER.

BEAVER

BODY LENGTH:
29–35 IN. (74–88 CM)

WEIGHT:
45 LBS (20 KG)

LIFESPAN:
ABOUT 20 YEARS

HABITAT:
CONIFEROUS FORESTS

THAT'S AMAZING!:
BEAVERS WARN EACH
OTHER OF DANGER BY
SLAPPING THEIR TAILS ON
THE WATER AS THEY DIVE.

MOOSE

HEIGHT AT SHOULDER:
5.5–7.5 FT. (1.7–2.3 M)

WEIGHT:
900–1,600 LBS (400–725 KG)

LIFESPAN:
UP TO 27 YEARS

HABITAT:
CONIFEROUS FORESTS

THAT'S AMAZING!:
MALE MOOSE HAVE LARGE
FLAPS OF SKIN HANGING
UNDER THEIR THROATS.
THESE FLAPS MAY BE USED
IN COURTSHIP.

MONARCH BUTTERFLY

BODY LENGTH:
1.3 IN. (3.5 CM)

WEIGHT:
0.02 OZ (0.6 G)

LIFESPAN:
UP TO 8–9 MONTHS

HABITAT:
CONIFEROUS FORESTS
(DURING WINTER)

THAT'S AMAZING!:
GENERATION AFTER
GENERATION OF
MONARCH BUTTERFLIES
SPEND THE WINTER IN
THE SAME TREES.

Find Out More

Books to read

Binns, Tristan Boyer. *Exploring Continents: Exploring North America*. Chicago: Heinemann Library, 2006.

Parker, Steve. *Life Processes: Adaptation.* Chicago: Heinemann Library, 2007.

Parker, Steve. *Life Processes: Survival and Change.* Chicago: Heinemann Library, 2007.

Websites

http://animaldiversity.ummz.umich.edu
The Animal Diversity Web is run by the University of Michigan and features an extensive encyclopedia of animals.

http://animals.nationalgeographic.com/animals
This website features detailed information on various animals, stories of survival in different habitats, and stunning photo galleries.

http://www.bbc.co.uk/nature/reallywild
Type in the name of the animal you want to learn about and find a page with several facts, figures, and pictures.

http://www.mnh.si.edu
The website of the Smithsonian National Museum of Natural History, which has one of the largest natural history collections in the world.

Zoo sites
Many zoos around the world have their own websites that tell you about the animals they keep, where they come from, and how they are cared for.

Glossary

adapted when an animal has special features to help it survive in its habitat

bird of prey bird that hunts for food using its talons

burrow hole in the ground or in a tree where an animal takes shelter

camouflage when an animal has special colors or markings that help it hide in its habitat

captivity animals kept in a zoo or wildlife park live in captivity. Animals in captivity often live longer than wild animals because they have no predators, nor is there competition for food.

coniferous made up of conifer trees, such as fir and pine trees, which have needles instead of leaves

conservation saving and protecting wild animals and their habitats

continent one of seven huge pieces of land on Earth

dam wall that holds water back

desert dry, sandy region

extinct when a type of animal dies out forever

freshwater water that is not salty, such as the water in rivers and some lakes

habitat place where an animal lives and feeds

hibernate to go into a deep sleep during winter

mammal animal that has fur or hair and feeds its babies milk

marsh land that is usually flooded with water

mate when an animal makes babies with another animal

migrate when an animal makes a long journey to find a better place to feed or breed

pollution waste, litter, and spilled oil that makes a place dirty and unfit to live in

predator animal that hunts and kills other animals for food

prey animal that is hunted and killed by other animals for food

reptile animal with scaly skin that lays eggs on land

rodent type of mammal, such as a rat or mouse

streamlined having a long, smooth shape for cutting through air or water

swamp area where large parts of the land are usually or always under water

talon bird's large, curved claw

Index